natural disasters

TSUNAMIS

Jil Fine

HIGH
interest
books

Children's Press®
A Division of Scholastic Inc.
New York / Toronto / London / Auckland / Sydney
Mexico City / New Delhi / Hong Kong
Danbury, Connecticut

Book Design: Dean Galiano
Book Layout: Jennifer Crilly
Contributing Editor: Jennifer Silate
Illustrations by Jennifer Crilly

Photo Credits: Photo credits: Cover, pp. 21, 24, 32, 36 © AFP/Getty Images; pp. 4, 7, 8 Getty Images; p. 11 © Japan Coast Guard/Handout/Reuters/Corbis; p. 14, 19, 28, 35 © AP/Wide World Photos; p. 16 kimimasa mayama/Reuters/Corbis; p. 22 © Jacqueline M. Koch/Corbis; p. 31 © Chris McGrath/Getty Images; p. 39 © Chaiwat Subprason/Reuters/Corbis.

Library of Congress Cataloging-in-Publication Data

Fine, Jil.
    Tsunamis / by Jil Fine.
    p. cm — (Natural disasters)
    Includes index.
    ISBN-10: 0-531-12444-4 (lib. bdg.)   0-531-18723-3 (pbk.)
    ISBN-13: 978-0-531-12444-4 (lib. bdg.)   978-0-531-18723-4 (pbk.)
    1. Tsunamis—Juvenile literature. 2. Indian Ocean Tsunami, 2004—
    Juvenile literature. I. Title. II. Natural disasters (Children's Press)

    GC221.5.F56 2007
    551.46'37—dc22

                                                        2006006246

1 2 3 4 5 6 7 8 9 10 R 11 10 09 08 07

CONTENTS

The 2004 tsunami destroyed many villages in Indonesia. Only rubble was left behind.

INTRODUCTION

At 7:58 A.M. on December 26, 2004, a violent earthquake shook the ocean floor about 150 miles (240 kilometers) from Sumatra, an island in Indonesia. It was the second largest earthquake ever recorded. The ocean floor was ripped apart for about 600 miles (966 km). Buildings crumbled on the island. People ran for cover and to help those trapped under the falling debris. The earthquake caused much damage and suffering. Yet the people on Sumatra and in almost a dozen other countries bordering the Indian Ocean were not prepared for what was to come next.

The earthquake sent billions of tons of water moving at speeds of 500 miles (805 km) per hour in all directions. The large, destructive waves created by underwater earthquakes and other natural events are called tsunamis. The first tsunami hit Sumatra less than a half hour after the earthquake. Survivors of the disaster said the water made a noise like a freight train as it approached land. The water surged up to 50 feet (15 meters) in some areas. It moved swiftly across beaches and through the city streets.

Banda Aceh, Sumatra, was the closest major city to the site of the earthquake. The tsunami moved with such force that trees, homes, cars, boats, and people there were swept away. The waters rushed inland and then back out to sea. Debris caught by the water crushed people in the waves' path. In just 15 minutes, tens of thousands of people in Banda Aceh were killed.

Over the next several hours, tsunami waves struck at least eleven countries around the Indian Ocean. Waves even hit Africa, about 3,000 miles (4,828 km) from where they had started. In total, hundreds of thousands of people lost their lives and millions lost their homes.

Since the Indian Ocean tsunami, governments and scientists from around the world have been working to better understand tsunamis and educate people so that another disaster can be avoided. Let's find out more about this deadly force, and what you can do if you are ever in the path of a tsunami.

The enormous amount of damage done by the tsunami made it difficult for survivors to find their loved ones.

The U.S. hospital ship *Mercy* sits in the water off the coast of Banda Aceh (top). It brought needed relief to the victims of the tsunami.

chapter 1

WHAT IS A TSUNAMI?

A tsunami is formed when an earthquake, volcanic eruption, landslide, or meteorite suddenly moves a large amount of water. A tsunami is not just one big wave. It is a series of waves, sometimes called a wave train. The waves are often only 1 to 3 feet (30 centimeters to 1 m) high in the deepest parts of the ocean. Sailors out in the deep sea may never even realize that tsunami waves are passing beneath them!

EARTHQUAKES

Most tsunamis are caused by underwater earthquakes. Earthquakes are caused by a sudden movement of Earth's crust. Earth's crust is made of giant plates of rock, called tectonic plates. These plates make up the ocean floor and the continents. The plates move about 1 or 2 inches (2.5 or 5.1 cm) each year. Over hundreds of years, the plates press against one another. Eventually, something gives. The lighter plate will sometimes be forced above the heavier plate. This sudden movement of Earth's crust creates an earthquake. Tsunamis are created only by this type of earthquake. A tsunami will not be formed if the tectonic plates split apart or slide past each other. It only happens when one plate is forced beneath another.

When such an earthquake occurs, it releases a lot of energy. Underwater earthquakes send water rushing upward, above normal sea level from where the earthquake started, or its epicenter. The rushing water becomes a tsunami.

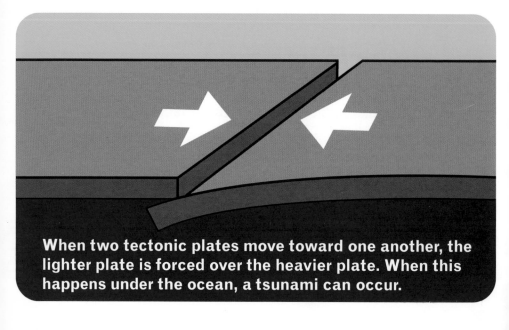

When two tectonic plates move toward one another, the lighter plate is forced over the heavier plate. When this happens under the ocean, a tsunami can occur.

Some underwater volcano eruptions can be seen by the towers of smoke the hot magma makes when it hits the water.

VOLCANOES

Tsunamis are also created by volcanoes. Volcanoes are openings in Earth's crust through which magma, the hot, liquid rock that is beneath the surface of Earth, and hot gases can escape. An eruption happens when pressure builds and the magma and gases are forced out of a volcano. If a violent eruption occurs underwater, it can release a lot of energy. The shock waves made from the release of this energy can cause tsunamis to form.

LANDSLIDES AND METEORITES

Tsunamis can also be the result of a large landslide or a meteorite striking the surface of the water. A landslide happens when huge chunks of land fall into the water. Often, landslides are created by earthquakes.

A meteorite is a piece of rock from space that enters Earth's atmosphere. If a large meteorite were to hit an ocean, the force of the impact could create a tsunami. No one has witnessed a tsunami as a result of a meteorite strike. However, many scientists think that a meteorite may have created a tsunami that wiped out life on Earth more than 3.5 billion years ago.

DID YOU KNOW?

The word "tsunami" has been used internationally since 1963. It means harbor wave in Japanese.

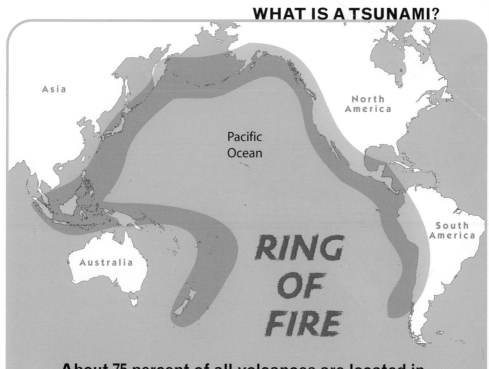

About 75 percent of all volcanoes are located in the Ring of Fire, shown in pink.

RING OF FIRE

There are several areas in the world where tsunamis often occur. These areas have a lot of earthquake and volcanic activity. One such area surrounds the Pacific Ocean. It is called the Ring of Fire. There are many volcanic eruptions and earthquakes in this area. This is because several of Earth's tectonic plates push against each other around the Pacific Ocean. About four out of every five tsunamis happen in the Ring of Fire.

A tourist staying in Thailand videotaped this tsunami wave as it approached land.

A TSUNAMI IS BORN

The millions of gallons of water moving from the site of an earthquake can result in many waves. There is usually a large space between the crests, or peaks, of the waves. This distance is often more than 100 miles (161 km) wide in the deepest parts of the ocean. There can be anywhere from 5 to 90 minutes between the crests of a tsunami. Tsunamis can travel more than 500 miles (805 km) per hour in the ocean. They can cross the Pacific Ocean in less than one day! After an earthquake, eruption, or landslide occurs, people often have only a few minutes to save their lives.

WAVES, WIND, AND TSUNAMIS

Regular waves are caused by wind pushing water at the surface of the ocean or other body of water. They can have quite a bit of force. If you have ever been knocked down by a wave at the beach, you have felt some of this force. Tsunami waves are created by an event that affects the entire water column, from the ocean floor to its surface. When that wave approaches land, all of that water builds up to become one very large wall of water. A tsunami wave hits land with thousands of times the power of a regular wave.

Only one building, a mosque, remained standing on this part of the coast of Banda Aceh.

chapter 2

THE ANGRY SEA

DISTANT AND LOCAL TSUNAMIS

There are two different kinds of tsunamis: distant and local. Distant tsunamis are tsunamis that are created more than 600 miles (966 km) offshore. Many of these tsunamis occur in the Pacific Ocean. Scientists have had much success predicting distant tsunamis in the Pacific Ocean. Distant tsunamis are far enough away from land that people generally have enough time to get to higher ground after being warned.

Local tsunamis are much more dangerous. Local tsunamis are created between 60 miles (97 km) and 600 miles (966 km) from shore. Landslides usually cause these tsunamis. Local tsunamis can hit land a few minutes after they are created. The Indian Ocean tsunami was a local tsunami for those in Sumatra and other nearby islands, but a distant tsunami in places

farther away. The people in Sumatra were not warned and did not have time to escape.
A local tsunami warning was made after the tsunami had already struck.

WEIRD WAVES

Tsunamis have been recorded at 100 feet (30 m) high. When the wall of water hits land, it may slow to about 30 miles (48 km) per hour. Though the first tsunami wave slows down a lot when it approaches land, it still has enough force to destroy. The fast-moving waves behind the first wave of a tsunami catch up to it as it nears land. These waves add to the force and height of the first wave as it reaches shore. The first tsunami wave is not necessarily the most dangerous. Sometimes, the waves that follow are more powerful.

DID YOU KNOW?

A 1958 rock slide in Lituya Bay, Alaska, created a tsunami that sent a wall of water 1,720 feet (524 m) high crashing onto the land facing it.

The 2004 tsunami caused about 750,000 people to lose their homes in **Sri Lanka.**

A tsunami's waves do not look like the waves that you might see at the beach. They do not break and curl as normal waves do. Tsunamis often come as rapid floods of water. The water quickly rises and floods an area several times.

Tsunamis can also come in the form of a bore. A bore is a large, steep wave that looks like a wall of water. It may have a churning, breaking front, but does not look like a typical wave.

Bores occur when a tsunami goes quickly from very deep to very shallow water. The wave is pushed up by the shape of the land to become a wall of water.

The places most in danger of being destroyed by a tsunami are those within 1 mile (1.6 km) of the shore and 50 feet (15 m) above sea level. When a tsunami hits, it can run up rivers and streets and reach far inland. Sometimes, a warning may come only minutes before a tsunami strikes. A tsunami moves so fast that if you can see it coming, it's usually too late.

DID THE ANIMALS KNOW?

Many people believe that animals can sense Earth's geological changes and know when an earthquake or tsunami is coming long before humans do. Hours before the Indian Ocean tsunami, people reported seeing elephants and flamingos heading for higher ground. Dogs and zoo animals refused to leave their shelters. After the tsunami, very few dead animals were found.

This picture of Banda Aceh was taken about one month after the tsunami hit the area.

People who study earthquakes use machines such as this seismograph to keep track of movements in the earth.

The Indian Ocean tsunami was a result of the most powerful earthquake the world had seen for more than forty years. It measured at least 9.0 on the Richter scale. The Richter scale measures the strength of earthquakes. An 8.0 or higher is considered a very powerful earthquake. The earthquake struck at 7:58 A.M. local time. Its epicenter was about 18 miles (29 km) below the surface of the ocean and about 150 miles (241 km) from the island of Sumatra.

The India and Burma tectonic plates had been moving toward each other for millions of years. On December 26, 2004, the India plate finally slipped beneath the Burma plate. The ocean crust cracked apart, creating a split more than 600 miles (966 km) long. Some areas of the seafloor were forced up as much as 50 feet (15 m). This movement sent water barreling outward in all directions. Most people had no warning and no idea how destructive this disaster would be.

Sadly, some people went onto the beach to see how far the ocean had gone out. Many of these people were drowned when the waves came in.

A CHANGE IN THE SEA

On the beaches of Thailand and India, the sea went out farther than anyone had ever seen before. Fish and boats were left helpless on the sand. Some people ran out to take pictures of the strange sight. Others knew that such an extreme change in sea level was more than unusual. It was dangerous. There were reports of people running for higher ground and telling

DID YOU KNOW?

There are so many tectonic plates on Earth that scientists have named them to help keep track. The United States is on the North American plate.

others to leave the beaches as well. The five-minute head start that these people got from the coming tsunami saved their lives.

THE MYSTERIOUS MALDIVES

The tsunami traveled to the shores of the Indonesian Islands, Thailand, India, Sri Lanka, the Maldives, and even as far as Africa and Australia. When the tsunami hit the Maldives, where the highest point is 7.9 feet (2.4 m) above sea level, very little damage was done compared to other affected islands.

So, how did these islands survive this disaster so well when they lie so low in the water? Scientists think that the coral reefs around the islands and the islands' low height above sea level protected them from the waves. The coral helped to absorb some of the energy of the waves. The low height of the islands kept the waves from building into 30- or 50-foot (9 or 15 m) waves as they did elsewhere. Eighty people lost their lives in the Maldives. If the islands had not been naturally protected, the tragedy could have been much worse.

WHEN WERE THE WARNINGS?

The people living around the Indian Ocean had no way of knowing that the killer tsunami was headed their way. There was no system in place to warn people of coming tsunamis. Tsunamis are much more common in the Pacific Ocean. There are several warning centers set up there to identify a tsunami threat. The Pacific Tsunami Warning Center was started in 1946 after a deadly tsunami in Hawaii. If the 2004 disaster had happened in the Pacific, the warning would have gotten out and more lives would have been saved.

In fact, the Pacific Tsunami Warning Center had picked up the earthquake in the Indian

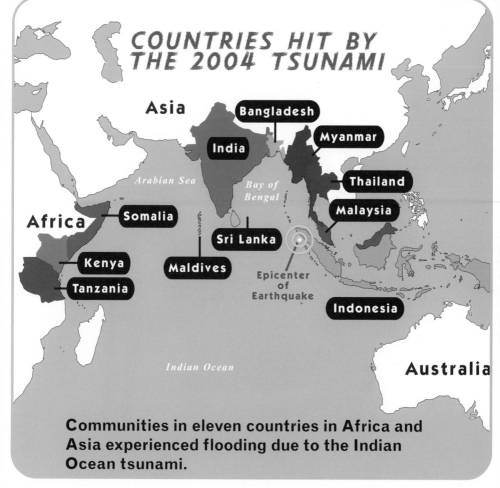

COUNTRIES HIT BY THE 2004 TSUNAMI

Asia

Bangladesh

Myanmar

India

Arabian Sea

Bay of Bengal

Thailand

Somalia

Malaysia

Africa

Sri Lanka

Kenya

Maldives

Epicenter of Earthquake

Tanzania

Indonesia

Indian Ocean

Australia

Communities in eleven countries in Africa and Asia experienced flooding due to the Indian Ocean tsunami.

Ocean. Workers there placed calls to Asia after the earthquake, but it was already too late. There was no system in place to get the news out quickly enough to the affected areas. The earthquake struck too close to land. By the day's end, the tsunami had taken the lives of more than 200,000 people.

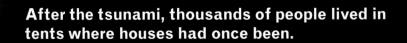

After the tsunami, thousands of people lived in tents where houses had once been.

chapter 4

CLEANUP TIME

There was much work to do in the aftermath of the Indian Ocean tsunami. Families were separated. Many children were killed or left without parents. Millions were homeless. The tsunami filled freshwater wells with dirty water and swept waste into the streets. The governments of the nations hit by the tragedy could not possibly help their citizens on their own. Organizations and governments from around the world sent aid workers to the areas in need. Donations given for the tsunami disaster were the largest ever made. About 13 billion dollars was pledged by countries around the world to help in the relief effort.

SURVIVORS

Many people who survived the tsunami were badly injured. Health organizations tended to those who were in immediate danger of dying before caring for people with cuts or broken bones. Many hospitals were destroyed, so healthcare workers had to make do with what was on hand until supplies arrived.

GIVING AID

Aid organizations and governments worked to get the money and supplies that were donated to those who needed them most. This turned out to be harder than expected. The governments of many countries, including hardest-hit Indonesia, did not have a system in place to make sure help got to those in need. Even when they could get aid to the right people, other problems arose. Some aid agencies rushed in to build new housing, but the agencies often chose poor building materials and locations. There was no plan for an emergency as big as this one.

Reports of dishonesty soon arose. Some people received a lot of aid, including money and new homes. Others got nothing but what they could find in the ruins. Many people had to fight to take back land that had been theirs before the tsunami. More than a year after the tsunami, governments are still working to

This memorial service was held in Thailand to remember the victims of the tsunami.

determine the safest location to rebuild permanent homes and how to give out the aid that was received.

Despite the difficulties, progress is being made. The huge effort is creating jobs as well as homes. Islands that once had a successful tourist industry are rebuilding hotels in the hope of attracting visitors once again.

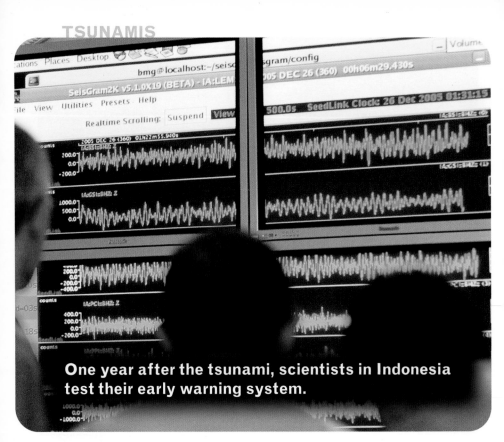

One year after the tsunami, scientists in Indonesia test their early warning system.

SETTING UP WARNINGS

The nations of the Indian Ocean are just as focused on preventing another tsunami disaster as on rebuilding. Part of the reason that so many people lost their lives in this tsunami was because there was no effective warning system in place. There had never been a tsunami disaster to compare to the one that took place in 2004 in the Indian Ocean. Since the devastation of the Indian Ocean tsunami, people are working to set up a way to warn those living there if another tsunami threatens.

Governments, international organizations, and scientists have worked together to develop a system to reach the communities on the Indian Ocean. The system includes a network of local communications to quickly spread the word of a coming tsunami. The Indian Ocean is also now monitored with the latest technology to watch for the possibility of another tsunami. These technologies are already in use in the Pacific Ocean. Even though tsunamis are more frequent there, the loss of life from a single tsunami in the Pacific has never come close to what the Indian Ocean tsunami caused.

FINDING A TSUNAMI

Special instruments called seismographs are used around the world to detect earthquakes and other rumblings within Earth. These tools measure the vibrations inside Earth's crust and rate them on the Richter scale. Since only a few earthquakes produce tsunamis, seismographs alone cannot accurately predict when a tsunami will occur. They can, however, rate how large an earthquake is so that scientists know when there is a possibility of a tsunami.

Scientists also use bottom pressure recorders to monitor the oceans. A bottom pressure recorder on the ocean floor measures the water pressure every 15 minutes. If something unusual is detected, it will measure every 15 seconds to gather more information.

Buoys are often used to measure conditions in the deep sea. A floating buoy sends its own data and data from the bottom pressure recorder to a satellite high above Earth. The satellite sends the information to scientists at watch centers around the world. This system is called the Deep-ocean Assessment and Reporting of Tsunamis (DART). It is used in the Pacific Ocean and now in the Indian Ocean as well.

Sea-level and tide gauges are also being used to detect tsunamis in the Indian Ocean. These gauges measure the sea level and tides at the shore. They were in the Indian Ocean before the tsunami, but did not send data regularly

These sensors will be dropped into the Indian Ocean to measure Earth's movements under the water.

enough to be useful. These gauges have been improved so that they now send data in real time to tsunami centers in the region. Scientists in tsunami centers now learn of changes as they are happening. The gauges are also getting an important upgrade. They'll use solar panels so that they will continue to work even if electricity is out.

GETTING THE WORD OUT

Most of the twenty-seven countries that border the Indian Ocean have now set up their own systems to alert people to incoming tsunamis. Some countries are using sirens along their shores. Others are broadcasting warnings on local television and radio stations. Most countries are working to educate their citizens

In Thailand, this officer is checking the tsunami warning system during a test drill.

WHAT DO YOU DO?

Hawaii, Alaska, and the west coast of the United States and Canada are also at a high risk for a tsunami. In fact, they've already had them! So what should you do if you are told that a tsunami is approaching your area?

• Know how high above sea level your street is and how far away it is from the coast.

• Make an escape plan for getting to higher ground and make sure that everyone in your family knows it.

• Have disaster supplies ready. Make sure that you have a flashlight, batteries, a battery-operated radio, a first-aid kit, and emergency food and water.

by holding tsunami drills, putting up warning signs, and teaching about tsunamis in schools.

LESSONS LEARNED

On March 28, 2005, just three months after the deadly tsunami ripped across the Indian Ocean, another violent earthquake struck near Sumatra. Tsunami warnings were given to those in the surrounding area. After feeling this earthquake, locals did not wait for the warning to run for higher ground. Fortunately, the plates only slid past each other and no tsunami occurred. If it had, the experiences and lessons learned from the events of December 26, 2004, certainly would have saved thousands of lives.

Today, scientists are working hard to figure out how to predict a tsunami. They know how they form, but not when or where they will strike. Through better prediction, education, and action, people hope that a tragedy like the Indian Ocean tsunami will never happen again.

This tsunami warning
system in Thailand will
make announcements
in six different
languages if a tsunami
threatens the area.

Europe

HISTORY'S EIGHT DEADLIEST
TSUNAMIS

North
America

North
Atlantic
Ocean

③

②

Africa

South
America

South
Atlantic
Ocean

⑧

① **Indian Ocean**
2004 **225,000+ deaths**

② **Crete-Santorini, Ancient Greece**
1410 B.C. **100,000 deaths**

⑤ **Krakatau, Indonesia**
1883 **36,500 deaths**

⑥ **Tokaido-Nankaido, Japan**
1707 **30,000 deaths**

Asia

North
Pacific
Ocean

Indian
Ocean

South
Pacific
Ocean

Australia

3 Portugal-Morocco
1755 **60,000 deaths**

4 South Sea China
1782 **40,000 deaths**

7 Sanriku, Japan
1896 **26,360 deaths**

8 Northern Chile
1868 **25,674 deaths**

NEW WORDS

bore (**bor**) a kind of wave that is large and steep and looks like a wall of water

bottom pressure recorders (**bah**-tuhm **presh**-ur ri-**kor**-durz) devices used to measure the pressure of water at the ocean floor

buoys (**boo**-eez) floating markers in oceans or rivers

coral (**kor**-uhl) a substance found under water, made up of the skeletons of tiny sea creatures

crests (**krests**) tops of something such as a wave or a hill

Deep-ocean Assessment and Reporting of Tsunamis (**DART**) a system used by scientists to monitor oceans and detect tsunamis

distant tsunamis (**diss**-tuhnt tsoo-**nah**-meez) tsunamis that are more than 600 miles (966 km) from shore

earthquake (**urth**-kwayk) a violent shaking of Earth, caused by a shifting of the crust

epicenter (**ep**-uh-sent-ur) the area directly above the place where an earthquake occurs

gauges (**gayj**-ez) instruments for measuring

landslide (**land**-slide) a sudden slide of earth and rocks down the side of a mountain or a hill

local tsunamis (**loh**-kuhl tsoo-**nah**-meez) tsunamis that occur between 60 and 600 miles (97 and 967 km) from shore

NEW WORDS

magma (**mag**-muh) hot, liquid rock found beneath Earth's surface; when above ground, it is known as lava

meteorite (**mee**-tee-ur-ite) a piece of rock or metal from space that enters Earth's atmosphere at high speed and does not get burned up in the process

predict (pri-**dikt**) to say what you think will happen in the future

Richter scale (**Rik**-tur **skale**) a system of measuring the strength of earthquakes

Ring of Fire (**Ring of Fire**) an area on the outer rim of the Pacific Ocean where there is a lot of volcanic and earthquake activity

seismograph (**size**-muh-graf) an instrument that detects earthquakes and measures their power

tectonic plates (tek-**tah**-nik **playtz**) large sections of Earth's crust that make up the continents and seafloor

tide (**tide**) the constant change in sea level that is caused by the pull of the sun and the moon on Earth

tsunami (tsoo-**nah**-mee) very large, destructive waves caused by an underwater earthquake or volcano

volcanic eruption (vol-**can**-ic i-**ruhp**-shuhn) a forceful explosion of magma and gases from a volcano

FOR FURTHER READING

Carruthers, Margaret W. *Tsunamis.* Danbury, CT: Franklin Watts, 2005.

Morris, Ann, and Heidi Larson. *Tsunami: Helping Each Other.* Minneapolis, MN: The Lerner Publishing Group, 2005.

Stewart, Gail B. *Catastrophe in Southern Asia: The Tsunami of 2004.* Farmington Hills, MI: Thomson Gale, 2005.

Torres, John A. *Disaster in the Indian Ocean: Tsunami 2004.* Newark, DE: Mitchell Lane Publishers, Inc., 2005.

Walker, Niki. *Tsunami Alert!* New York: Crabtree Publishing Company, 2006.

RESOURCES

ORGANIZATIONS

National Oceanic and Atmospheric Administration
14th Street and Constitution Avenue, NW
Room 6217
Washington, D.C. 20230
Phone: (202) 482-6090
Fax: (202) 482-3154
http://www.noaa.gov

Pacific Tsunami Museum
130 Kamehameha Avenue
Hilo, HI 96721
Phone: (808) 935-0926
Fax: (808) 935-0842
http://www.tsunami.org

RESOURCES

WEB SITES

FEMA for Kids: Tsunami
http://www.fema.gov/kids/tsunami.htm
Learn about tsunamis and how to prepare for
one on this Web site. Also, see dramatic photos
of tsunamis and play a tsunami-related game.

National Geographic Kids: Killer Wave!
Tsunami
http://www.nationalgeographic.com/ngkids/
9610/kwave/
Find out more about tsunamis and read a first-
hand account from a survivor of one of these
killer waves.

USGS Earthquake Hazards Program—For
Kids Only
http://earthquake.usgs.gov/4kids/
Read earthquake trivia, play games, and solve
puzzles on this in-depth Web site.

INDEX

INDEX

ABOUT THE AUTHOR

Jil Fine has written more than one hundred titles for children. She is a member of the Society of Children's Book Writers and Illustrators.